STALLION OF A DREAM

ROBERT VAVRA

STALLION OF A DREAM

Library of Congress Catalog Card Number 80-82431
ISBN 0-688-03746-1
Color reproduction: Cromoarte, Barcelona
Printed in Germany
First Edition
1 2 3 4 5 6 7 8 9 10
Designed by John Fulton

This book is dedicated to the memory of Majestad.

It will be long before there is born, if ever,

An Andalucian so frank, so rich in adventure;

I sing your elegance with words that moan

And remember a sad wind among the olive trees.

Federico García Lorca

INTRODUCTION

Photography's initial incursion into the world of painting began with portraiture; those splendid unblinking moments captured every wrinkle in unpressed trouser, every inflection of bonnet and ribbon, every jowl, every crease, every wayward hair.

Of course, to commission a portrait of the boss, even one that bore only a wooden resemblance to the sitter, was for long considered slightly more dignified than a lifelike photograph, simply because it was considerably more expensive.

Who would have thought, in those early days of sepia and white, that photography would, very soon, acquire a palette of its own, and invade the provinces of impressionism, abstraction and surrealism? That it would, in fact, possess a wider field of expression than painting, since there are certain mysteries attached to its manufacture, at least to the layman, and some of its effects are miraculous as dreams, as nature itself.

Robert Vavra is one of these artists, part magician, part alchemist, who is able to take a simple pretext, like the mutual attachment between a gypsy boy and his horse, and create a series of photographs that illustrate, or rather illuminate, this attachment in a series of unforgettable compositions. The book is a kind of rhapsody on a theme often redolent of the poetry of García Lorca, and therefore of Spain itself. Pride fills these pages, sometimes expressed as a gentle, almost reticent arrogance, sometimes as a wild challenge to soil and sky, to human or animal possibility itself.

Perhaps it is true to say that this collection of poetic fragments expresses the most necessary and most underrated of virtues, that of respect. The mutual respect between boy and horse, and eventually the respect of the boy for the liberty of the horse, are philosophical attitudes of great beauty and great subtlety, artistically concealed among the more obvious attractions, the blinding fields of flowers, the jagged silhouettes of rock and grass, the tremulous pallor of the moon, and everywhere, majestic in the foreground or barely visible, like hints, like oversights, the heads of horses.

In fact, a book such as this needs no introduction; a word of praise would be sufficient. Anything more is like a coughing fit in a cathedral or, sometimes even worse, the voice of a guide in a museum. Suffice it to say that the boy is called Federico, like García Lorca, and the horse is called Majestad, like a king. Even if the avid pulse of the guitars and the raucous voices of primeval pain are not far away, they are out of earshot. Only audible are the whinnying and neighing of horses, the occasional cry of night birds, and the low voices of poets; only visible are the dunes and marshlands and vast sky, the boy and the horses, the epic intimacy of Robert Vavra's vision.

PETER USTINOV

STALLION OF A DREAM

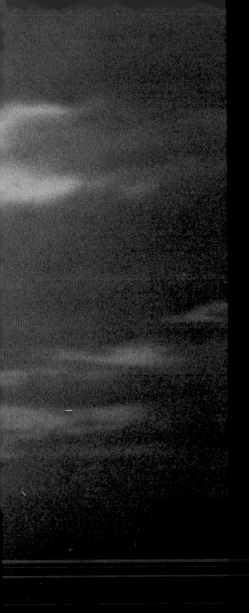

The moon in open spaces lit,

Horse of the quiet clouds, is

showing...

A lad as graceful as a reed

With shoulders broad and body slight,

With skin of moonlit apples,

Sad mouth, and large eyes brimmed with light...

Federico García Lorca

With a white stallion

the youth began to dream

until one day he caught

it by its mane...

Antonio Machado

Look, what a horse should have

he did not lack,

Save a proud rider on his back.

William Shakespeare

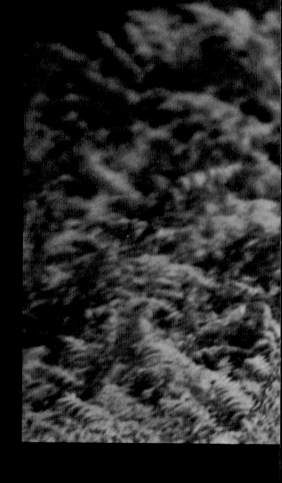

The back of thy horse subjects the world to thee.

I will fashion it into a throne for thee;

whence thou shalt wield a scepter of power, of joy

and freedom, such as is beyond expectation.

Rudolf G. Binding

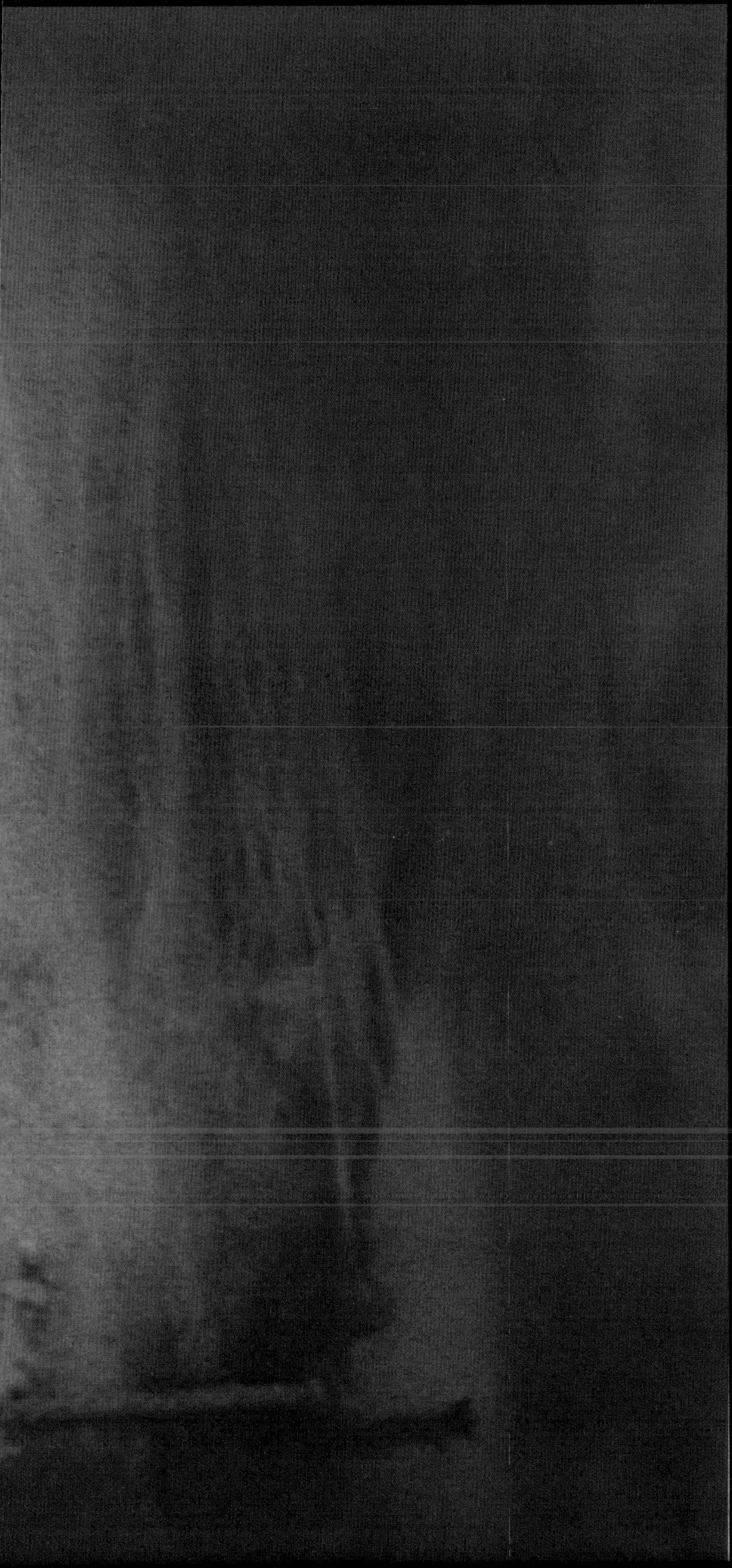

All the treasures of this earth

lie between thine eyes. Thou

shalt cast Mine enemies beneath

thy hooves... This shall be

the seat from whence prayers

rise unto Me.

The Koran

Before me peaceful,

Behind me peaceful,

Under me peaceful,

All around me peaceful—

Peaceful voice when he neighs.

I am Everlasting and Peaceful.

I stand for my horse.

Navajo song

My horse the dolphin of the plain

My boat of roses, steed of fire,

At once the courser and the shallop,

He came into my life as the warm wind

of spring had awakened flowers, as the

April showers awaken the earth. My

love for him was an unchanging love,

high and deep, free and faithful...

Anna Chennault

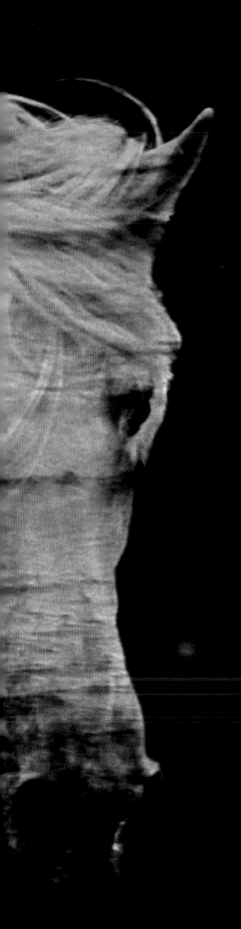

There is pleasure in the pathless woods,

There is rapture on the lonely shore,

There is society, where none intrudes,

By the deep Sea, and music in its roar:

I love not Man the less, but Nature more...

Lord Byron

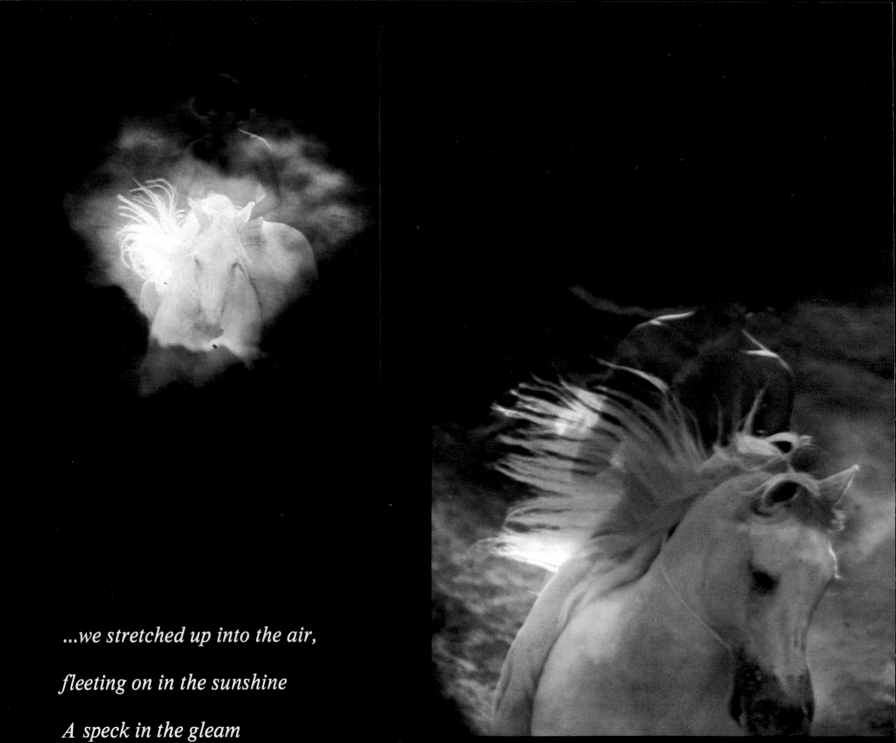

...we stretched up into the air,

fleeting on in the sunshine

A speck in the gleam

On galloping hoofs, his mane

in the wind out-flowing

As if in a dream.

Walter de la Mare

Fear is not the contagion of sorrow

When evening falls

And the sunset stains with blood

The muddy seashore,

The lands, and the sky,

Until these isles are swallowed up in shade...

Fear is the dread that you might go

And leave me here alone.

Joaquim Paco d'Arcos

To be a horse!

To know that freedom

and run with them.

I would have given anything

to be a horse!

The Count of Odiel

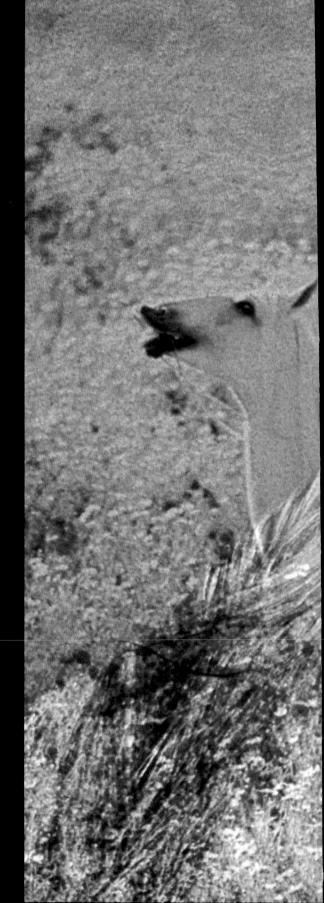

A ll the world was mine

until

the day he lifted

his head to call—

but not to

me.

The answer he awaited

could only be

another neigh.

Robert Vavra

Round the cape asudden came the sea,

And the sun looked over the mountain's rim:

And straight was a path of gold for him,

And... a world of men for me.

Robert Browning

My hand forever in your mane so dense,

Rubies and pearls and saphires there will sow...

Oasis of my dreams, and gourd from whence

Deep draughted wines of memory will flow.

Baudelaire

How could you expect me

Farewell! a word that must be,

and hath been—

A sound which makes us linger,

—yet farewell!

Lord Byron

But...

Nothing in the world is single;

All Things by a law divine

The earth's pollen rises as they pour out,

The shining dust of the earth covers the

horses' bodies,

As I become one of them.

Navajo song

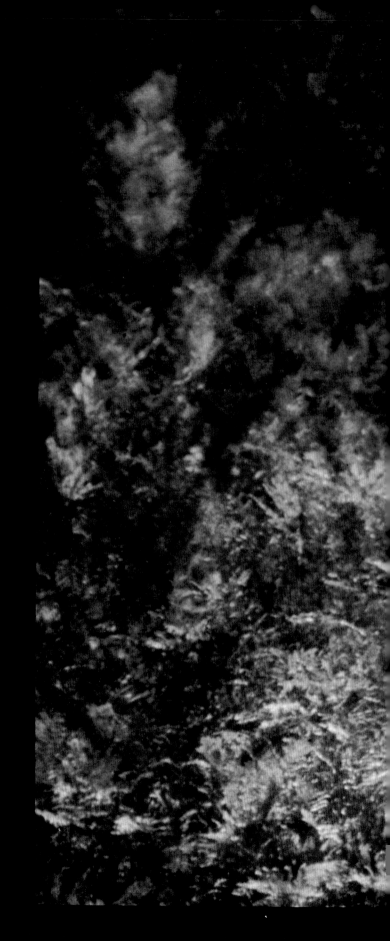

As I become one of them.

Like the Most High Power Ways are

beautiful so are horses,

As I become one of them...

Navajo song

You see, I am alive.

You see, I stand in good relation

to the earth.

You see, I stand in good relation

to all that is beautiful.

I stand in good relation to you...

You see, I am alive, I am alive.

Kiowa song

AUTHOR'S NOTE

Author's Note

The photographs for this book were taken prior to 1976, some time before I had started to focus my attention on horses, a course of work that later led to Equus *and to* Such Is the Real Nature of Horses.
What inspired Stallion of a Dream? *As a child I had always dreamed of being a horse, and though I had never been able to realize my fantasy, a book seemed a good way of giving some other youth the opportunity to do so. Federico, the gypsy boy who had served as the protagonist for my books* Milane *and* Romany Free *(set to paintings by Fleur Cowles), was then sixteen years old and seemed just right for these photographs. And Majestad, who was owned by Federico's father, John Fulton, was indeed the stallion of a dream.*
Those were wonderful days, working with them in the marshes and on the clean-swept dunes of the Coto Doñana, a wildlife paradise in southern Spain. Never have I been so touched by an animal — and I have worked with many — as I was by Majestad (pronounced Mah-hay-stahd and meaning Majesty). Besides being a stallion of such beauty, he was at the same time kind, noble, forgiving, and, in a mysterious way, strangely distant which made him even more attractive. Without his patience and goodwill, this book would never have been done. In the Coto Doñana he was worked not by expert horsemen, but merely by three humans who loved him very much.
Majestad touched, as deeply as he did me, everyone who had the good fortune to know him. In the film The Last Remake of Beau Geste *he was ridden by the fine American actor James Earl Jones, who in several letters to John Fulton expressed his desire to buy the horse and to take him to America, saying that never in his life had he been so moved by any living creature. It was at this time that Peter Ustinov became acquainted with Majestad and Federico. Every year in the Sevilla Fair, when John rode his white stallion among thousands of other equestrians mounted on the finest Andalusian horses, it was Majestad who attracted the most attention.*

Well past his prime when these photographs were taken, Majestad was in fine condition and had a youthful spirit. Some Spanish breeders felt that his head was too long for a modern Andalusian; however, it was that very longness of head which, combined with his noble eye, made him even more appealing and romantic, reminiscent of the medieval horses that prance the paintings of Madrid's Prado Museum. It is unfortunate that the reader could not have seen Majestad in movement, for he had such a high lift to his forelegs that he appeared to have been trained to walk that way.

Although the photographs for this book were finished years ago, I had a difficult time with the accompanying text. Everything I wrote seemed to describe the images too closely, failing to generate any life between the two. It was only after I had finished Equus *that I decided to use quotations for* Stallion of a Dream. *The task seemed a difficult one — using the words of writers of all nationalities and periods of history to tell the story — but in my reading I found that though their language differed, many authors, from Shakespeare to a Navajo Indian, shared the same sensitivity in their treatment of the two themes of the book: horses, and love.*

In part it was Majestad who was responsible for the rebirth of my interest in horses. He was the stallion that I used on the cover of Equus. *It might be said that he was born for art and that he died for art. In the fall of 1977 I had taken him to an area just south of Sevilla for another shooting session, and it was there that he suffered a bad fall. Ten days later he was dead. I cannot describe the sorrow of those of us who were close to him. But our sadness was soothed in some degree by the knowledge that Majestad would continue to give joy to people all over the world. Happily, many persons have been thrilled, as I had been, by the sight of that white stallion in his field of red poppies, the picture that has appeared in books and magazines and on postcards, greeting cards, notepaper, calendars, posters, puzzles, and as limited-edition prints in art galleries.*

For as long as I could remember, his field each spring had been a mass of red blossoms. Since Majestad's death, not a single poppy has sprouted there.

Acknowledgements

First thanks go to John Fulton, Federico's father and Majestad's owner, for the hours that he devoted to this book, especially to its design.
Paco Lazo, Antonio Romero and Miguel Angel Cardenas, three rancher friends, also provided valuable assistance.
Javier Castroviejo has my thanks for allowing us to work freely in the Coto Doñana.
Elias Garcia of Cromoarte, who made the color separations, and Rudolf Blanckenstein helped by expressing their continued belief in this project.
I am deeply grateful to my friend José Franco for his enthusiasm and assistance.
The photographs were taken with two Nikon F cameras equipped with motor drives, a 50 – 300 Nikkor zoom lens, and a 28 mm wide-angle lens. The film used for all of the photographs was Ektachrome X forced developed to ASA 160.